Ho! Rumpelstiltskin

NEW WRITING No 1

A COLLECTION OF POETRY AND PROSE
BY EMERGING WRITERS

Fighting Cock Press

CW01390407

Published by:

Fighting Cock Press
2 Vernon Road
Heckmondwike
WF16 9LU

Editors: Mabel Ferrett and Pauline Kirk
Marketing: John Ferrett
Finance: Geoff Kirk

Printed by Peepal Tree Press

Typeset by Pauline Kirk
Design and Layout by Geoff Kirk

Original 'Fighting Cock' design by Stanley Chapman

ISBN 0 906744 14 8

SUPPORTED BY
THE NATIONAL LOTTERY
THROUGH
THE ARTS COUNCIL
OF ENGLAND

CONTENTS

FOREWORD

A mapping of our world: that may serve as a simple metaphor for an anthology of contemporary writing. Naturally, we shall expect to find in such a volume features a little different from those provided by our estimable Ordnance Survey. Here we may anticipate by contrast cities of the mind, resignposted legendary trails and inset cross-sections of layered meaning.

From Lesley Quayle's vigorous retelling and refocusing of Rumpelstiltskin to Jez Colclough's dramatic fragments of a passionate relationship, a narrative impetus informs the poetry as well as the occasional prose of this anthology. Perhaps that is a specific task of the writer in the late twentieth century - to construct new stories when the grand narratives seem to fail us. The 'stories' told here cover diverse territory to map the dense networks and diffused energies of contemporary life. So on the one hand John Walker and John Carley, though as different from each other in mood and imagery as Cotman and Turner, both renew the indispensable links of nature with human nature. On the other hand, Jean Barker embodies for us that most mundane and amazing of modern Odysseys - that of the 'ordinary' family and individual through a century of emigration, war and social upheaval. Then Helen Clare points us forward to our possible future (wondrous? disturbing? definitely both) of Californian entropy.

I needed to mention such names to convey the specific strength of this collection. More just as worthy could be cited but in order not to be invidious I stop here - at the point where most that interests me in the anthology must go unmentioned. The majority of writers here demand to be judged by the best standards of technique: and even if in certain cases this high proficiency is not achieved one feels the writing's active, interventionist energy challenging the reader. If this anthology provides a showcase where lesser-known writers old and new can display their talents, and if it grants the reader at least a handful of voices that stay in the memory (and I believe it will do both) then it will have justified its existence. But, to return to my opening metaphor, I think it does more, in that its writers map a number of the key journeys of the spirit that most of us must undertake towards the imminent millennium.

Ken Edward Smith

HO!
RUMPELSTILTSKIN

Lesley Quayle

Ho! Rumpelstiltskin

Consider a man,
father, peasant,
dreamer,
arms thick as an anchor rope,
bearing his shoulders like a mountain range
above his oaken back;
this barge of a man
whose hands worked like a team of oxen,
had the brain of a hen,
had a daughter,
beloved doll child, rocked asleep
on the voyages of her father,
becalmed on his oceans, lit by the fastened moon
of his tender gaze,
promising kisses for the nape of her neck.

Consider
a king, not young,
not yet old,
a solitary man
with a heart empty as a cracked cup,
eyes like cigarette burns
in the rice-paper skin of his face.
Gold worshipper,
lover of shining coins,
sifter of yellow dust.
This king, who roams his realm by night
listening to the crushed whispers
of his subjects as they squeeze together
in the loving dark,

2

his heart hushed as a museum,
hears rumours, borne on the rank air,
of a beautiful daughter
who spins hay into gold.

Consider
a mannikin,
cockroach, froglet,
spat from an appalled womb,
dropped and abandoned,
wet nursed at goblin breasts,
greedy suckler of the rancid, magic milk,
pumped up with its poison
from his spider legs to his humpback,
which he carries like a sack of stones.
Hides in the secret depths of the forest,
away from the mother eye of the village
where ordinariness fêtes itself,
lovely as ripe strawberries,
sweet as honeysuckle.
Rumpelstiltskin, little scorpion brain,
ugly, pinchfaced, kiss-me-not of the gloomy forest,
hears a sobbing swelling through
the night like a symphony.

Consider,
a vaulted room, locked and bolted,
stuffed with the harvest of two sweet meadows
and a spinning wheel beckoning.
The peasant's daughter,
cobwebbed skin, cheeks soft as kisses,
weeps;

for herself,
for her worm-brained, chanticleer of a father,
crowing like a clarion
of a beautiful daughter spinning hay into gold.
The foolish boast, fluid as a snake,
flickered an enticing tongue
into the ear of the gold-hungry king
who seized the girl (noticing her marigold hair
which swung to her waist like a wide river)
and offered a bargain, as kings were wont then.
Marriage for gold,
death for hay.
And now her sobs pierce the silence,
are carried to the covert lair of Rumpelstiltskin.

Consider this.
Rumpelstiltskin,
his withered heart plumped by pity
appears in her prison,
but what will she give him in return for his magic?
She regards the hunchback with his wish-bone legs,
rodent eyes and thin smile,
offers him her pinkie ring and the trade is set.
All night, while she sleeps,
he spins the fragrant stooks to gold,
ryegrass, meadowsweet, buttercup and ox-eye daisy
fed from his flying fingers to the humming wheel.
At dawn, the king's men unbar the door
to find her, a sleeping beauty, lying among the yellow threads
like a wren in her nest.
The king's burning eyes devour the treasure

and if the peasant's daughter dwelt
pleasantly on royal marriage,
it was only because she was innocent
of kingly company.
Another, bigger room was furnished with the harvesting
of seven meadows,
a state of the art spinning wheel,
an orthopaedic chair, to spare her back
and the same terms as before.
As he locked her in, the king found himself consumed
by pale blue doll eyes and rowan red lips.

Consider her tears.
Consider the hump-backed,
lumpbacked,
spindle legged hybrid,
her hob-goblin saviour,
spinning all night in return for the seed pearls
which nestled against her white throat.
At dawn, the king ordered the doors
to be opened without a sound
so that he could look at her sleeping,
cradled in the skeins of gold.
Then he gave an order for the harvesting
of every field in the kingdom,
every blade of grass from lush pasture
to parched scrub,
scythed and turned, dried and baled,
delivered to the castle.
The peasant's daughter begged his pardon,
and the arid heart of the king grew love
like maram grass.

"Once more then marriage."
Such is the arrogance of kings.
The palace swelled with bales and stooks
as the livestock withered on stubble
and farmhands predicted a winter of death.
Locked in with the hay and barely room
for the state of the art spinning wheel
and orthopaedic chair,
the peasant's daughter waits with bovine patience
for the ugly little spinner of gold.

Consider
her dilemma
when the question is mooted,
and what will she give him,
how will they trade?
The Brothers Grimm fudge reality to spare parents blushes.
She simply does what peasants' daughters have always done
when their backs are up against the wall,
hoists up her skirt invitingly
and shuts her eyes.
The frog-goblin,
malformed fleshling
with his insect genitals,
shudders over her and is quickly spent.
She smiles politely,
even hob-froglings have egos to protect,
smooths her ragged petticoats and waits for him to spin.
"One more thing." His smile curls like an asp.
"I want the child."
An easy one, she knows you can't catch the first time,
(her father surely doesn't count,

at least that's what he told her when he crawled upon her
thick as pond weed).
She promises, cross my heart and hope to die,
lies down to dream of cathedrals and choir boys,
of thickets of rose petals, dense as snow.

Consider
the wedding,
the clamorous bells,
such pageant and pompery,
gold coach and high stepping stallions,
alleluias of the starched choristers
with their perfect 'Os' and pious eyes,
the long walk down the aisle
on the arm of her father, subtle as a cattle prod
in a hired penguin suit,
then the hi-jinks of the crowds,
throwing rice and white roses,
their joy more potent than a sniff of opium.
The king regarded his new and lovely queen
and,
having great palaces stuffed with gold,
was content to treasure her over all things.

Consider a pregnant queen,
ripe as a pear with her belly moon
slung round her hips,
breasts nuzzling the rim like two fat piglets.
As she spreads her legs wide,
straining like the old house cow,
blowing into her cheeks, unpacking throat noises
with gathering abandon,

this peasant-queen screams for release,
for the chicken skulled spinner of gold
to eat her pain as her bones stretch
and the child's head blooms in blood at her thighs.
The king, in his chamber, is told by his secretary,
told by a footman, informed by the wet nurse,
selected by the midwife, of the uneventful birthing
of an exceptionally healthy son.
Rumpelstiltskin tastes the tart air of daybreak,
scents a stranger, naked as a trout,
swallows a tear from liquorice black eyes.

Consider a summer evening,
brown moths skim the candle flames,
curtains pant from open windows
and the royal son sleeps,
pink snail, thumb-sucking peacefully.
Rumpelstiltskin arrives.
"Lady, keep your word, I have come for him."
The queen trembles, pale as flour,
cold as moon, screams for her guards
but the cry chokes her throat like sherbet.
Exquisite, she offers jewels, riches,
scratches up brocade skirts and silk petticoats,
wears martyrdom like a crown until
his angers boils, thick and fermented as sour milk.
"You promised. Give me the child."
Now she is lost, suffering for innocence,
compromised by father, king and terrible dwarf,
picked and pressed, melted down and poured into a narrow mould,
her raw, red wounds buried in smooth, harmonious flesh.

Her tears are parasites to a halfling's heart,
burrowing into the dull middle,
biting like firecrackers on the deadened tissue,
eating it like hot kisses till he relents.
"Three days, three nights to guess my name - and,
if you do you keep the child."

Consider the first night
when she goes from Adam, Aaron, Art
to Zebediah, Zorro, Zak,
piles up slag heaps of names before him
until his neck aches from shaking his head.
Night two:
crates of books shipped from far flung kingdoms
with continents of names, unwrapped hopefully
before the triumphal leather-jacket, little sour-skin
salty fellow, sprat with a secret.
"Have mercy." Rumpelstiltskin is oiling his tongue
for a night of saying no and has no truck for mercy.
The queen sends her listeners, gatherers of indiscretions,
crouchers under the window sill,
bated breathers in open doorways,
rodent scufflers beneath the bed,
even with the crowd sounds turned up full volume
can discern the fall of a feather,
the footfall of a mouse on grass.
The day unwinds a hot white sheet of sun,
wraps the trees in lightsails like the masts of tall ships
as the queen's listeners trawl the shadows for secret shoals.

Consider one,
pressing his ear to the moss skin of the forest,
with its dry earth throat, and hearing,
above the voice of the throbbing river
and the green pool, rising like a dead eye,
a different song.
"Merrily the feast I'll make,
Today I'll brew, tomorrow bake,
Merrily I'll dance and sing
For next day will a stranger bring:
Little does my lady dream
Rumpelstiltskin is my name."

Consider how he runs through the deepening dark,
deaf to the whelping vixen and the red, rutting stag
to tell the queen.
Then came Rumpelstiltskin, clad in silk,
dancing round the crib like a jester,
white faced puppet on a stick,
hard on the hot heels of the forest eaves-dropper.
"What is my name?"
"Archelaus, Athelstane, Auberon or Hector?
Clarence, Clerebold, Conal, Conan, Finn?
Hardwin, Hector, Melchisadek or Victor?
Or, let me see, are you Rumpelstiltskin?"
Scarecrow man, rag faced, with your smile
stitched like a scar and your boot black eyes
grown small as poison berries,
the peasant-queen has won her child.
Rumpelstiltskin brings up curses,
spews rivers of anger from grey lips,
tears drop like dead flies

as he circles the cradle.
His name sours the tongue of the peasant-queen
and she bids him go.

Consider the passing years,
a prince, now eighteen,
orbiting the palace like a death star,
mother's-apple-of-my-eye, huge baby-mouth
sucking her dry,
bleaches his black hair white as ash,
tattoos flaccid skin with hollow eyed skulls,
swastikas, black hearts a-bleeding,
no ornamented "MOTHER"
or rose-wreathed heart.
Pierces nose, ear lobes, lower lip and tongue
(and other tender parts long since pricked)
with eighteen carats.
Close clips his purple goatee-beard,
re-arranging gaunt features to a
satyr mask,
his liquorice black eyes sinister as flint;
bad meat, maladjusted as a Nazi.
The king, considered a man
without imperfections,
examines carefully hidden cancers,
worries that they might be growing, unchecked,
in his son.
The peasant-queen loves her soiled princeling,
drawn up out of hell, with his hands
like pitchforks and his long, straw legs,
to rupture her heart until she wears her pain
like a second skin.

Rumpelstiltskin, forbidden father,
banished from the tribalism of family
and friends,
rooted among bark and bones,
abandoned by nature,
stirs his fire,
exotic red and orange in the blue/black night,
and waits for the footfall of the stranger.

FROM

CALIFORNIA NOTEBOOK

Helen Clare

San Francisco - First Impressions

Here you can paint your house purple
practise Tai-chi in the park
holler at squirrels;

you can drive a Dukes of Hazard Dodge
raise your jeep on stilts
knit in restaurants;

you can cross-dress roller blade
call to strangers
joke with gun toting policemen.

The city has already given its permission -
asks only to be celebrated.

Nob Hill, San Francisco

The houses here are a bright confusion
of spa town hotels

opera houses   inside out
Swiss chalets   plastered in geranium pink

Parisian bordellos
gothic castles   curved glass in turrets

Greek temples   in Byzantine shades
of topaz and lapis lazuli

cowboy film façades
built in wood   leaved in gold

14

Bolinas Beach

At first the mist wipes away
only the base of the landscape ahead,
like polish on a picture glass
but as we walk it rises,
dissolves away hill and sky,
until all is gone,
but one small dark Corot tree.
It scrolls beside me
up buddleia-covered sandstone slopes,
rolls behind and soon
just the dark frond edges of the sea are left.
There is nothing now,
but mist, the sweep of the sea, cold sand
between my toes.

Your call cuts through
You have spotted a sign - *Groin,*
pose grinning, knees splayed.
I snap.

Sitting on a Ridge, Muir Woods

In front of me:
a valley,
a forest,
a ridge, a road...

.... the Pacific Ocean.

Behind me:
a ridge,
a forest.....

...... two and a quarter thousand miles......

the Atlantic.

A beetle hurries past my left foot.

Giant Redwoods - Muir Woods

Treetops converge
to a feathery beanstalk world
of contrast.
Only in death
do they tumble
to our comprehension.

16

Freeway

You explain you need to drive this fast
for changing lanes. Signs rush past -
an impenetrable forest. Our hire car -
a compact - is dwarfed by trucks. We are
lost, alone depressed beneath a California sky,
on unforgiving tarmac. "Which way now?" you cry
and I reply, shuffling the acres of paper on my lap
"Which way, he says, which way... which map!"

Mexican Restaurant, Santa Cruz

There's a man in the corner, who, baseball cap apart,
looks like an extra from a Spaghetti Western,
The man behind the counter looks familiar too,
maybe it's the white hair, the wiry spectacles,
the gap toothed smile, the way he shuffles
to the tables, keeps his pen behind his ear.

Childish peasants gaze, wide eyed from wooden plaques,
but the lamp - a resin sun-god does not shine.
Photos of the 'Giants' plaster cobalt painted tiles
and tongues of plastic hibiscus tease the air.

In the other room, somebody plays the piano
badly. The South Pacific train rattles the plates.

Sea Nettle, Monterey Aquarium

To be of water, and in water
to feel light and filter light
to glow golden, and pulse
with the immemorial urge
of sea and sun,
to drift, and then ride
the rush of currents,
for the wordless self
to extend
through vapour trails of tissue
the length of hair-like threads
and beyond,
through progeny
that dust the tides.
To kill swiftly, die,
and not fear death.

California and Kierney

Chinatown gateway,
red and gold pagoda.
Double yellow arch,
over McDonalds.

Yosemite, First Impressions

Seems to me this is Sunday best country.

Ain't like weekdays, mud and sweat,
food and drink country.

It's white veiled virgin country

> Ain't a woman you could lie with
> touch the belly of;
> ain't for rolling or soiling.

Ain't even Friday night kicking up dust country.

Not even Saturday morning
whistling on the way to the stores country.

It's like the Lord,
I can't reach out and touch.

Cozy Bear Cottage, Yosemite National Park

Inside the blue cottage, there's every home comfort
you don't have at home - dishwasher, waste disposal
a basting pipette. In the kitchen there are four bowls
of silk flowers, ducks on the crockery, cows on the linen
and teddies where there's space. One or two ducks, cows,
escape the blue gingham and lace, wind up in the blue chintz
(and lace) of the lounge. But the lounge is the province
of the bears: ten in all, in picture, plaque and fur.
The largest sits upon a wicker throne above
the glass fronted log fire. Bears, ducks and cows alike
avoid the cerise chintz and satin patchwork
(and lace, and silk flowers) of the bedrooms.

Outside the sugar pines litter the still torn earth
with giant cones. There are no grizzlies here.

Yosemite: removing the cellophane
Instructions dictated by an imaginary lover

1.   Avoid giftshops, visitors' centres, museums
Do not read notices attesting to the triumph
of nature and the park committee.
Leave maps and guides in the bag.

2.   Lie down.

3.   Watch the bug, busy in the chickweed,
the ponderous droop of the pines.

4.   Follow their reach to the skyline
where trees as tall, huddle like cake decorations
on the last remains of winter's snow.

5.   Resist the temptation of mental arithmetic
as regards height.

6.   Instead consider that it is we
who are small, low, and that all size is relative
and therefore unimportant.

7.   Briefly remember the bug.

8.   Believe the eye is a tentative finger.
Let it follow ruts and arches,
rub over shadows.

9.   Then, close your eyes.

10.   Allow the sounds of birdsong
and falling water to invade your sleep.

Stanford Linear Accelerator:
Song of the Stanford Electrons

*Electrons are accelerated by riding
the electro-magnetic wave - like a surfer
on a water wave.**

We are the man, the board, the surf
the tide, the sun, the moon, the earth.

We bind the water to a mass
prevent its dissolution into gas.

Ours is the urge, the need for breath.
Corruption, the slow slide into death,

is driven by our desire, our spin.
The illusion of matter, the space within,

is our domain, but substance of your earth.
We are the Universe.

Today, we ride your wave.

*Display Board, Stanford Visitor's Centre

On the Bus to Golden Gate Park
The Hair of the Negress

Ebony would be a cliché, and despite the sheen
and the smell of strange oils, the curls like burrs
inaccurate. It is too fluid.
It is like glass, never truly solid.
Like the blown and twisted glass
of a goblet stem, miraculously separated
and lying layer on layer
heavy and still. And yet not still.
Like the mane of a horse
it remembers movement, air,
is finely balanced like the lascivious anthers
of tulips offering sooty pollen to the wind.

She shakes her head, and in a moment I miss
it dissolves into a thousand strands and then reforms.

San Francisco - The End of the Affair

This morning, stepping out of Embarcadero
I smelt sewage. The dust stung my eyes.

And then the Polish Waitress
a good city if you have money...
... five dollars an hour...
a quarter to the taxman.

I let you touch me,
wore a fresh dress every day.

FROM

PEARL OF THE ORIENT

An Autobiography of a Mid-Fifties Army Service
in the Far East

Duncan Earl Smith

Singapore

On my arrival at Changi Airport, I was very impressed by the unfamiliar shape and outline of the buildings, bamboo trees in abundance amidst a heavy undergrowth, swathed in the light of a brilliantly waxing moon, all draped in a hot and humid blanket.

With the deafening sound of innumerable insects, predominated by the high-pitched whine of the mosquito, came the pungent fragrance of wild flower and tree blossoms we could never hope to know - a very heady cocktail for five humble soldiers to assimilate; all we could do was stare about us in curious surprise.

Our world of translucent imagery was suddenly shattered by the sound of screeching brakes as a dark green mini-bus came to rest. As the driver's window went down we were confronted by the grimacing face of a small Malaysian soldier, dressed in the normal olive green uniform, but wearing a black fur-like busby, surmounting a rapscallion gold-toothed grin. Did he know something we didn't, I thought, as we scrambled aboard?

We were soon to find out for the moment we sat down the bus shot forward at an incredible speed and above the sound of bated breath could be heard the driver's demonic laugh. Now we knew the reason for his jubilant grin. He got his kicks from scaring people half to death.

Now, careering along a single dirt track road, through an endless sea of jungle picked out by the headlights, we maintained our unnerving dash with the driver's face still creased in delirious mirth.

It seemed we were going to a transit camp some twelve miles away at Nee-Soon although nobody had bothered to inform us officially. We only found this out between outbursts of hysterical laughter from the driver.

Our arrival was just as spectacular as our departure had been; one quick dab of the brake and we all shot forward spilling out into the road, disgruntled, but still pleased to have arrived without mishap. Although it was still dark we could just make out the shape of what appeared to be native huts on a steep hillside. We were told they were our new quarters and generally referred to as Basha's.

We quickly reported to the Camp Office which was no more than a thatched hut and were checked in by a perky cockney Corporal of the Royal Fusiliers whose regiment had long since left, but he remained at his own request, having married a local Malaysian girl. He told us half his life story as he issued us with all the necessary webbing, eating irons, drinking mug and a set of bedding, including the mattress. Concluding his business, he wished us well and ordered two men to help us with our extra kit.

Of the two men who came to my assistance one was a Gurkha who could not speak much English, the other an Irishman who appeared to suffer from the same affliction. Nevertheless, they were both friendly and cheerful companions. The Gurkha quickly hoisted my mattress and bedding upon his head and started up the hill at a cracking pace. The Irishman regaled me with his exploits on Christmas Island, from which he and the Gurkha had just returned and how he was looking forward to going home in a couple of hours time.

As we continued to climb the hillside together Michael talked in a very excited manner, giving snippets of advice and one theme he harped on incessantly, long after we had reached the Basha, stressing all the time in a strong Irish brogue:

"Do not pay more than two dollars for a jump in Singapore for that's the going rate." He repeated this statement over and over like some deeply profound wisdom as he shook my hand in farewell.

Our goodbyes said, I set about finding a suitable bed space and sorting my kit out in readiness for the day's work although, being new to the unit, I had been granted a further two hours to put my kit in order.

This gave me a chance to take a closer look at the Basha. One of the first things I noticed was its seeming frailty for it was entirely made up of bamboo canes interwoven with broad leaf foliage and fibre and held together with dried clay.

The windows were glassless arches, much appreciated at present with temperatures in the region of eighty-five degrees Fahrenheit, but I found it difficult to imagine what it would be like with a force nine gale blowing, or a monsoon in full spate and I had heard that such things were not uncommon in this part of the world.

I was soon made aware of the numerous ants, both red and white varieties, that were entrenched in the parquet flooring and, of course, the omnipresent mosquito.

Standing in the centre of this long, dark, green-leafed room and listening to the chirping sound of lizards that ran rapidly in a zig-zag fashion on the exposed roof rafters, or sitting staring with bulbous eyes, patiently awaiting the arrival of the unsuspecting mosquito, I felt myself witness to a timeless vigil as, once again, a green lizard flicked out its swathing tongue to pick off yet another mosquito in full flight.

In these unguarded moments of dreamy, tranquil bliss there lies more danger than that of a simple insect bite for within these walls, or in some dark, secluded corner, a Bamboo Snake may lurk, and also the dreaded Boot Lace, a snake that generously grants its victim a four-minute life after the one and only bite. I was pondering these thoughts and observations when my quiet calm was shattered by the voice of Derek Larkin whose accent never failed to remind me of broad Norfolk acres. Now, standing in the doorway, he excitedly urged,

"Jim! Hurry up! They are all waiting for you at the Company Office. The Sergeant Major's there, sorting out the work parties."

EVERY LIFE A TREE

Margaret Wainwright

Photographs of My Mother

First: a costume photograph to us -
long, heavy skirt, black bun -

away in the days before we were,
before her marriage even, another world:
Jessie Charlesworth, severely black and white,
as a maid, an undoubted treasure.
She looks refined and serious, a bony face
not expecting too much, chasing dreams,
perhaps, but never out loud,
preoccupied with younger sister's welfare,
now they are left motherless, and concerned
for her employers, too.
          I know her now,
as I did not, when, long ago, the studied pose
first caught my eye.

Then: this second photograph to me was Mother,
as she had always been, must always be.
Thin as a stick at the picnic in the park,
wearing that knitted beret, hands outstretched
to catch my baby sister if she fell.
         I knew her then
          and know her better now:
one who never asked for more
than at that moment we could give,
but gave herself unstintingly.
One who, as we grew, became our friend,
with no transition felt,
One who, in quarrels, was a source of peace.

And so to these:

> her Indian Summer, after sixty,
> Dad had retired and we had jobs at last,
> and they could go on tour every year
> and bring back happy snapshots
> of Scotland or the lakes, never abroad.
> She put on weight, and pleased herself -
> that short, belated spell.

And now:

> every birthday means a photograph with flowers.
> Almost she seems weighed down with flowers,
> being thin once more, and bird-fine.
> Happy snaps are taken amid loud trivia:
> 'Farewell', on each side, breathed without a word.

For John Clare

At five, not knowing what you dared,
You went to find it in that outer landscape,
The end of the world - a dozen fields away.
The flowering earth, flat as a carpet,
You thought would simply stop and from its end
You'd gaze into the blackness of the void.

Rustling in summer hedges,
Scents, twitterings,
A songbird's lonely sweetness,
The warp and woof of nature closely seen
Displaced such cloudy images

Till Time
Within the landscape of the mind
Sweet folly of childhood turned to truth.
And we remember you
For minor, charming country tunes,
But most for that most piercing cry:
"And yet I am - I live - though I am tossed
Into the nothingness of scorn and noise."

Sad poet, would it comfort you to know
How straight your arrow flies across the centuries -
How deep it bites? Or would you still
Choose rather your sweet childhood sleep,
Before the void had meaning?

34

Hoccleve's Chaucer

"Dear Mayster and Fadir"

There is a portrait by Hoccleve, his friend.
Chaucer is seen as an unworldly poet, still
dressed without fashion or brightness, in black.
His deep-set eyes seem fixed upon some other scene.
His welcome is gentle but distant;
Hoccleve wonders whether the portrait is just.
He smiles, remembering Chaucer's younger age.
What pleasure it was, he thought, remembering,
the talk, the mimicry and irony.

But Chaucer was a listener, too, though then
his ears were sharper and he could extract
any unstated implications
while like a chessman he counted his own moves.

Chaucer to some was an unproven spy,
imprisoned for some years in France.
The only evidence of innocence might be
the patronage of low and high;
kings, too.
Hoccleve was touched with friendly jealousy.

Factory

Thin black vertical pipes
rising to
multifarious pipes below the roof
(They carry gas and air).
Rooted grey or green machines,
smooth and squat at the base,
blossoming metallic and spiky
into levers, handles, knobs and assorted
movable parts - an inelegant jungle.
It's not light, not dark.
In the roasting summer the glass pleats of the roof
were mercifully painted green.
But the air is stale whether hot or cold,
and strip electric lighting
replaces the sunshine
down the bare stone walls.

The people clocking in accept
this one out of many
possible servitudes,
cheerfully (You've got to have a laugh)
or grumpily, as their nature dictates.

The pay's the thing (though always too little)
the skill also, sometimes.
It's not all that bad, the factory!
You can wear ear-muffs against the noise,
and, of course, eye shields,
and with care you shouldn't
lose a finger end.

The eye, searching, finds
the allure of the shining metals worked upon,
copper and brass and silvery alloys,
shiny as mirrors,
their beauty accidental to their uses.
It finds also
the freedom of the flames,
the quiet, yellow, waiting flames at dinner-time
when gas jets are left on.
It finds
a romance of destination, China or Nato -
parts from this bench, our bench, circling the world.

And when this is not enough, there is always
clocking out.

Continuum

Time stirs his hand a little, spreading fingers
wide, and out spills Rome. See Christ arise -
Mahomet and Napoleon, Karl Marx,
some Ghengis Khan that's still to come,
and still to trickle from his cloudy grip.

Time gives his judgment for their rise or fall:
sees generations run to death, and sees
their hopes blown helpless on his gales astray
Remote, unheard,
bird voices streaming backward into time
cry out "We never meant"... "We could not guess"...

Their protest whirls away.

Mining

Mining always sounded so hard,
and riddled with chest complaints,
but soft, too, like *How Green was my Valley*,
full of free coal and a spot of housing.
There was pride under the softness. A back-to-front
pride in surveying hardships from history, and some
from today. Plenty of great brass bands and speeches, too,
socialist, of course, or communist perhaps.

One sunny day I sat outside the small
local library, waiting for a pupil.
Occasionally, I glanced across the square
to the Miners' Retirement Home to see
their beautiful small skyscraper.
My pupil came. We had our lesson.
Afterwards we walked among the trees, mature
or nearly so, and widely spaced: Man's work
not Nature's. But suddenly we came
to a small plaque with thirty names perhaps,
a memorial to miners who had died
in a pit explosion.

Every Life a Tree declared the plaque,
as if it were wartime still.

Refugees

The crowds are settling down,
setting out cooking fires,
stealing from our Aid waggons,
or tracking a muddy, slippery stream
from which cholera springs.

I got all this from the telly last night.
Today it sounds worse.

No-one in the city starves, so why
that high, unearthly wail?
Children, not present, but felt presences,
skeletons walking unsupported. Eyes
that seem bewildered since the grown-ups fail.
My bucket weighs heavy. It feels the fallen
forest, the soil that turned to dust
to make us pretty luxuries.

Our streets fling plagues and then
their victims trail implacably across our T.V. screens.

Pity and panic rise from souls long untried.

Night

Illuminated, pleasuring Night! Neighbours
hastening to pub or disco in cars,
or taxis, or on motor bikes or buses find
lights brighter within its frame of black.

Shift workers yawn and ignore its neutral shades,
its power blotted out within the walls
of factories, fire stations, hospitals.

The city slips like sand between the fingers.
A girl is short-cutting so late across the Park.
Is it a dog in the bushes? Is it ...?
We are waiting for disaster, long foreknown.

It is the hour of loss; the year of failing.

The homeless see now, straining at blackness,
an ancient, muzzled enemy, let loose.
Wheezing tramps facing long hours
in wet and roofless houses, tilt the bottle;
drain the last pale, fiery, useless drops.

Yet morning comes as obstinately as night.
Time stirs his hand and on his waiting stage
dance groups of children, ignorant and fearless,
laughing because the world's made new for them.

GROW THERE, MY HOPES

John Walker

Undone Again

After you've noticed it's not the same this time,
the snowdrops, catkins, crocuses et cetera,
slipping by,

then calmed yourself,

before the full-blown signs you're now not looking for,
(no daffs burst open; hawthorn just whitey buds,
no tufts of green)

it catches you off-guard again,
yerks its stiletto under the ribs with,
this year,

two mallard,
necks craned,
wings blurring,
wheeling off the wood edge,
over February's slops,
the flooded ings,
4.25 p.m. and the light holding.

Out in the Flooded Ings

A child's face appears above the wall,
looking down for footholds, not at me,
though she climbs in confidence I'm there.

Hooded for the wind and rain, she seems
as keen to hunt the flooded fields as I,
not trailing after my desires, hers usurped.

She tops the wall, for once above my height;
her eyes look down at me, mine up at her.
Then, arms stretched scarecrow-wide, she launches out,

part lean, part clasp, part fall. My right arm sweeps
around her waist, swings, then lowers her to ground.
She clings a moment, then begins a smile

to give us both away. I turn aside.
"Come on!" I say. "No dawdling! We've more floods
still to find." She slowly moves away

and I stand still and wait for her to turn,
ten years before the card that I must own for mine,
the only words upon it "From Janine".

Jim Allen Lane

"...............................*fifty faggots*
That once were underwood of hazel and ash
In Jenny Pink's Copse. "

Straight from an Edward Thomas poem,
Who was he, then, to have this named his lane?

Eccentric, centenarian, philanthropist?
The grasping holder of the fields each side?
One who loved the lane and haunted it?

No need to hunt his memory from its resting place.
The local habitation and his name have fused
Around the strange fact of a life.

How much identity's to be had with earth!
And how much love - when things go well.

The great but linger in the memory.
I'd settle for his one bright spark of fame,
This sign a living shrine.

At Appleton Roebuck

What was that noise?
Oh, what was that noise?
And where was it, where?

It stopped me from walking.

"It's only the wind in the telephone wires,"
My father's voice said.
"Did you hear the foxes barking last night?"

I never did hear them the week we were there,
In a real gipsy 'van, leaking rain in a corner.

But I did hear the sound of the wind in the wires,
A wild, hollow thrumming and shrilling.

How did I know that this was the loneliest,
Emptiest noise in the world?

Something had told me if I got lost,
No-one would find me.

And the wires were singing it.

The Ice Mountain

The children called it that three quarters of a century ago,
in Norfolk, near Old Buckenham,
a sort of mound or rise as she described it,
covered in white violets.

Going to gather purple ones to dress the church for Easter,
you smelt them on the breeze before they could be seen;
and primroses so thick you couldn't see the grass for yellow.
Oh, yes, and in the fen, keep to the path your only warning,
orchids, so many orchids, one place a solid patch,
big as a carpet.

Where was The Ice Mountain?

You went beside the church and through two fields,
then struck across another.
But would the path and stiles be there?

"I'll go," I thought, before I knew it,
the name Old Buckenham,
fast as seven sevens in my mind.

But if you never found it?

Well, you'd known you never would.

And if you did?

A glory for the moment?
No more than wonderful?
For, seeing how the afternoon wore on,

where is the village house you'd run back to,
your mother there, watching her bread,
saying abstractedly, "Oh, there you are!
How long you have been out!"
then, brightening, "Oh, how lovely!
I'll put them into water right away"?

I'll let myself go look,
her memories like seeds
dropped in my head.

Snowprint

Faint but perfect,
the feathered impression of grouse wings
in the blank snow of the moor,
the take-off moment printed.

One of my boot clumps had clipped a wing.

It would not have lasted, anyway,
this print of white on white,
so light the impresssion where
air kissed earth goodbye.

Cheyney is Fit

"Devouring time, blunt thou the lion's paws"

Stubborn, desk-top graffiti.
Brown-sweat drops on the sander's dust.

Why this one so deep?

Depth of impression from depth of impression,
Or,
Dull lesson, sharp point and strong arm?

Whatever,
As ever,
Scored on the present's surface,
The endless urge to live on,
Here doubly seen.

Un-human, then,
Obliterating,
With grains of sand.

Hopeless, too:
Someone scrawled as I toiled.

A low-down scribble to the end of time
Had us shadowy effacers beat.

But that's partial, too.

It's all reassigning.

Dry Walling

Pick and lift and try and fit
And settle and chock all day.
Stone scritch-scratches the rough glove.
You invent descriptions for the one you want:
Thin in-squeezer; flat-long narrowy; square clumper
With a corner lifted like a curled lip.
A heap of stones is a feast of choices;
Stone running thin frays the temper.
When successive stones fly to their places,
You're in tune that day.

Not that there is a perfect fit.
Doubt comes with the compromises,
But endurance grows with the wall.

By mid-stage,
Footings long buried,
First throughs a memory,
Top stones over the horizon yet,
It's in the blood.
You hear the chuckle of the hearting trickling in,
And, travelling home, feel more tired to see
Miles of walls on the moors, some broken down.

But heaving on the copings is play,
A rejoicing that hardly tires,
However long it lasts.

In Farrar's Stoneyard

Large sandstone blocks lodge in Farrar's yard.

Torn from the quarry wound,
dumped from battered trucks,
they smell of the moor.

Silent,
unmoved,
unmoving,
power squats in them,
an exact fit.

Single,
exposed,
they long to be as before,
buried,
undivided.

Over life-size,
blank bulk,
their faces are what's inside,
compacted matter,
blocked mass,
weighting down gazes,
fronting stares.

Stars

I have seen stars
through bare black branches
slipping between the arms
of their tormented and hopeless lovers.

I have seen stars
engulfed by clouds
re-appear much later
quite unharmed.

I have seen stars
distorted and fragmenting
in the waters of the earth
gather their pieces.

I have seen stars
so thickly clustered
the night sky seemed ablaze,
singing its own magnificence
and needing no-one's praise.

I have seen stars
singly and timidly appear
in the tender paling sky,
shy lights within the shell of dusk,
looking as though the dark
would put them out.

Willow

You've a good soft bed under your roots.
I saw to that.
I dug deep and threw the stones out.

The long root,
I stretched west,
Where our wind is from,
Then heeled the soil back hard.

Your hand-span stem,
I fastened firm to a stake.

Our wooden seat-swing,
Fixed on its end next to the wall,
Made you safe from browsing cows.

In the late dark,
In the early morning,
I went out to you,
Made anxious by the wind.

My cares now whisper,
"Grow there, my hopes."

TURNS AT TYDAVANET

Josie Kildea

Turns at Tydavanet*

If I hear the Ink Spots singing
I am there, in the dip near the flax field
Under instruction, winding the gramophone
Anxious the game won't change
Before my turn for the dancing

The machine, carried by cousins
With just two records, my other family
And I over for the long holiday
Barefoot, delighted, a stranger, in spite of
My dad one of them and
Knowing the Gaelic

Even their first names
Made mine sound heathen
They'd strength in numbers
But it was the dancing
That channelled the gap
Too wide between us

They in a line, with straight ahead gaze
Legs flicking from knees
Familiar precision, finger tipped thighs
Seemed to me then,
Like soldiers dancing

If I got my turn after all their fiddling,
There was need to move fast
Swaying and curved to the sonorous
Blues, so fluid and foreign
The beat bent into sadness,
Miles away from their jaunty tunes

Sometimes now, in the awful news
Of what goes on in the gaps,
Between the flax field and the country road
I think of those cousins long gone,
Their fiddles and mouth organs mute,
There's enough of my father in me
To smart at the old unfairness.
I am anxious again,
With a much longer view,
That the game won't change,
And always the soldiers,
No longer dancing

* Pronounced TEEDAVANET: Name of farmstead in
Co. Monaghan just inside/bordering the free state.

News from the City

Those Christmas Days before,
When the structure of our life
Unfolded, according
To whose feed it was
Instead of the Queen's speech
You made your telephone call to Bristol
The name sprang into image
The arcs of steel suspended
Above the dark wide river
I would hear you in the cold hall,
Warmly aarring and rolling round the family news
A young John Silver recovering himself
Greeting the pirates.
You'd return to the kitchen beaming, not a duty done
But a homecoming, by proxy.

Whenever we went on visits
The shoe box car, polished and packed
With children and their clobber
That bridge beckoned
Your silver acrobat, cartwheeling across space.

Christmases went and came,
Until that Spring and
The telephone call from there,
To you, changing everything.
There are few clear cards,
In the deck of memory, but
I can see you, feel you now,
Your strong frame shaking,
And the bridge
Stopped being Bristol.
Even now, a newsflash
Or a photo of it
Makes you wince,
As if you want
To bandage up that place,
Hurl it down the rocky gorge
Along the Avon,
Bruising and hurting
Into oblivion,
Like your brother.

In the Flax Field

In the flax field I learned
What it was to be foreign.
We played hide and seek
As the grown ups stooked
And the dry dust rose.
Then, over beer in bottles
And billy canned tea, they
Told tales of old Uncle Oiney
Who'd married and moved
To America, returning fast
For the very next harvest.
We sat on stalky ground
Munching our soda bread.
They'd strength in numbers,
My cousins who spoke
With a voice I lacked,
I longed to be like them
Tried to keep up with their
Legs, their laughs, their history
They got tired of it often,
Pushed me through thorny gaps
Of their Border field.
Holding me there,
Close to the spiky edge,
They'd taunt, "Go back!"
And with a final shove,
"Go back now, to England."

Poetry Reading

What am I doing?
Flattening my fins
On the sides
Of this glass-sphere
Dizzily swimming this way?
What has possessed me?
Thinking my thoughts
Will pass muster with
Other more seasoned mackerel
Who've been here before
Know how to exhibit
Themselves. Gills
Breathing beautifully
Scales iridescent
Whereas
I feel filleted
Already.
Won't it be ghastly
If I don't blow the right bubbles
Get tangled up in the algae
Just sink like
A very dead fish
Right to the
Bottom of this tiny tank
And lie there
So
Very still.

Remembering my Father

After you died
It took me half a lifetime
To observe convention
Track down some stone
The imprint of a carver.
He came to meet me
Sat across the kitchen table
While the setting sun streamed
Scarlet and the smell of supper
Heralded the task.
A big man, shiny faced, with
Huge shoulders, more stevedore
Than artist, until he spoke of what
He loved, the properties of stone
Its cutting texture and how
He'd never been abroad
Much less to real Carrara
Though the place, he said,
Existed in his head and
On his invoices from Italy.
As he lingered over wine
Moving his mind and fingers
Over the design, he
Grew purposeful,
Said he'd like to do
Work for people
He could get to know.

I gave him words
And he worked with these
Placing and replacing them
Across the rounded shape
I'd set my heart upon.
The pattern of letters he
Translated into spacing
With his carver's eye
So unlike yours and
I guarded the meaning
Of my message, with
Its small Celtic cross,
Centring the circle of birth and death
On grey-green Yorkshire stone.
Now twenty five years on
From when you died
It newly reads, "Nothing
Is lost. All is harvest."
I felt I was quite sure of that
Before the carver came,
But when I see this marker
Of your life, and mine,
I grow less sure.

At the Braque Exhibition

I heard colour sing today and
You were the missing flute
So necessary for the full orchestra.
You'd have loved the paintings,
Rich chrome yellow in the centre
Purple, olive and sage green
Planes of coral, cream and grey.
There's nothing so intoxicating
As colour, its warp and weft
Making shadows from solids,
Objects into shadows.
You'd have liked the artist's frugality
Rarely leaving his home
Looking and looking more at the same thing,
The discoveries of a lifetime in one studio
The big bird alighting on the canvas
Albatrossing white or black across the space
Above the intricate map of a cubist view.
It made me think of your absence
The time we lost when you were gone
After years of being cured, you said,
"They took away my colours,"
And afresh I understood
At the concert of colour today
When I got drunk on Braque.

Winter Walk

Coming early
a different way
at the top of the slope
we reached new country
and Turner's palette
of mists and marvellous
watery spaces. Beyond
were bell tower trees
and those small bursts of
sunlight, fiercely focused.
Below and across the
pale glistening hues
scores of waterfowl
slid like small craft
on their lagoon. While
at the water's edge
moored in their grandeur
were stately swans.
It took our breath
to find Venetian magic
with such swift ease.
As we walked on
transported in our luck
the mist lifted and
when we came to rest
you showed me
the earliest snowdrop.

Stolen Walk

Instead of feet in dutiful places
We set off on a secret walk
Surprised by swans, whose wings
Were louder in flight than
Schooner sails flapping
While the winter sun
Warmed our backs as we talked
And laughed unexpectedly
At a man who smiled as
He carried his multi-coloured
Umbrella. Up, in the dry
Of the late afternoon
Down the damp paths and
Across the marsh field
The tension dissolved
Like the recent snow
And left signs of the
Spring reappearing
And promising all
Things renewed.

THE FIFTY BUS

Alex Shaw

SLAM on the Bridge

The echo of the pointed kicks,
And the ball against the bridge bricks (bridge bricks).
Us playing SLAM.
Smashing the ball into oblivion.
Together we win the league for Leeds, in our dreams.

Soon it'll be next season. They might do it in reality.
Then we won't have to dream as hard.

But if not then there's always the season after......

So many seasons.

The bridge. Where time stands still for us to play.
Brothers, forming "good old days".
Yet we stand above the river, the canal, the train track.
Flowing water reminds, train roars can't be ignored.

At least there's the canal, the moat around our castle of static time.
Thank God it doesn't flow.

(But are there not boats?)

And how come I'm starting to look up at you, baby brother?

Yet still we play.
I sold the telly, and while others watch Saturday night dross,
We play SLAM.
And read stories.

Once we read about zombies; the dead who keep living.

Will we still play SLAM when we're dead? You ask.
"Maybe," I say. "But now let's get some games in,"
(Before the river forms another ox-bow).

Plastic Mac Love

I asked you to wear my love while I wasn't there.
I hoped it'd help you -
Help you feel secure,
if you weren't sure, that I cared.

But like a child, you hurried from sight,
Tore off my attire,
Went out with more fashionable loves -
To indulge your current desires.

To you my love is like a plastic mac -
Needed but unattractive.
But when there's a downpour in your mind -
Back you come,
On it goes,
To shield you from descending woes.

The Fifty Bus

They say that there's no point washing the rickety Number Fifty buses that travel through the council estates of Leeds. Nobody ever complains, apparently, that they can't see out of the windows.

Who would listen to "them" anyway?

It seems that the approach of one of these "dirt bag" buses, as they're known, acts as an early warning for the rather rich shoppers of the Victoria Quarter to avoid the set-down points and go for another Arabica at Harvey Nics. This, of course, is rather than to end up being confronted by the "vagrants" filing from the Fifty.

When I was a child, my mum used to point to the people stepping off these grimy vehicles.

"That", she would nod "is what will become of you if you don't keep your head down to the desk. You'll be a thick scruffer." If I didn't look sufficiently terrified at this point she would add "and I'll give you no pocket money if your next report's not good enough."

At this, of course, terror did ensue. I never really knew for sure, however, what point my mum was making. I never realised that these people even looked scruffy, and what it had to do with keeping my head down puzzled me. Things like that were always a mystery. Like Oxbridge. This place was never on a map, but seemed exclusively reserved for me, until one particular school report eradicated its existence. It was, however, quickly replaced by a place called Durham. This one was on the map though, and so not quite so exciting.

As I grew up, I began to realise that somehow my mum's middle-class mission had worked. Every time I saw someone who looked scruffy I would immediately think "get back on your Fifty to Hawksworth." I did also make it to University, even though Durham and a few other locations had to come and go first.

I once ended up on the Fifty bus. Feeling quite superior, I kept my head up high as I mounted the stairs to the top deck. A few derelict faces glanced up at me between surreptitious smokes as I sat down; their dole-darkened eye sockets making even the youngest face look old.

The windows were dirty and it irritated me that nobody seemed to care, but then they all had their heads down anyway. Maybe they didn't want to see the outside world. Maybe, I had thought, they really were ignorant and stupid like my mum was always saying; too stupid to realise that the world was worth looking at. I felt as though I wanted to enlighten them.

At this point, I really was feeling superior, and took out my 'Western Philosophies' book.

I became aware of a man staring as we neared the city centre. I became aware of his filed-down features facing me. He glanced firstly at the philosophy book, then me.

When I looked up he smiled knowingly, in a sort of wizened way, his tree-bark face opening to reveal a tobacco-blackened mouth.

"Go to University?" he asked.
"Yes" I replied, proudly.

He turned away, still with a reassured, knowledgeable look.

It wasn't until he was getting up to leave the bus that he spoke again.

"Aye" he said simply, "they'll learn you what they want y' t' know," and he was into the street in seconds.

Glacial You

When we try to embrace,
I slide off your icy surface,
And then you flail your frost,
At me.
But if you thawed I'd only fall through and sink.

Fall into you
Drown in you
Dissolve

- Please stay cold.

FROM

A SONG OF COMMONALITY

John Carley

Spring: Piercy.

Time is here indifferent, down Piercy Meadow and Paradise Street. Sunken sets encrusted with tarmac vanish inexplicably amidst ancient allotments, Japanese bind-weed, and casually anarchic rabbits.

Coarse beyond hope, windows blinded by breeze-blocks and wire, the ravaged mills sit astride their brilliant sluices, straining up at fantasies of cowling and copes, dreaming of soot.

There above the terraced banks where solitary herons hunt rainbow fish, set full square in iron bands, squat chimneys rise from the copy-book naze in proof of the mason's theorem.

Between thick walls of prodigal waste, iridescent fractions of oil soil the scene of furtive consummations: eyes agleam in penumbral chasms; fugitive fags on fire-escapes.

Tenuous sunshine filters the scent of puddings and aftershave, diesel on toast. Though sparrows scream outrage at immigrant starlings, the ginnels and entries and back-to-backs salute the passer-by.

Spring: Chapel Hill.

Around a paddock, in Barbour and britches,
rich men's daughters canter their hunters.
Passing pedestrians panic a Porsche,
and the Disneyland version of rural community
bulges with bankers in Wellington boots.

Tumbled embankments
are bound up with snowdrops,
and primroses curl in the crinkley furls.
Muddles of by-ways are puddled with marl,
and the blue blades of daffodils
dance by a brook.

Up Chapel Hill the dunnocks dart,
and jaunty jackdaws bounce about.
The air is quick and bright with calls,
but hunger haunts the hawthorns,
and the hedgerows offer only spines
and bitter bracts of beech.

In pastures bruised by frost and hooves
the cloven ewes crop close.
Not for them the masquerade
of goldfinches or four-by-fours;
instead they watch the alder,
seeing purple tips begin to swell,
knowing that the season comes
when buds and catkins thicken.

Summer: The Museum.

Stunted as the dowry
of a self-made moralist
the bare-faced building smugly sits
and dares the plebs to enter:
barred about with date stones
of the Bethels and Bethesda's
that the feckless generations failed to fill.

Braided scarlet cables
rope-off gilded candelabras,
glitzing walnut inlaid uprights
like a stage for Liberace;
brass-plate grates could satiate
a plumped-up Father Christmas,
but the portraits of the patrons
are bereft of all goodwill.

The corridor leads grimly
to a charnel-house of taxidermy,
gruesomely precogniscent
of Belsen-Birchenau.
The children's eyes grow wide
before a pitiful Orang-Utang
whilst adults seek to comfort them
with tracts of down-right lies.

Upstairs is the shrunken head
- a souvenir of Ecuador -
and Accrington escapements,
rare as craters on the moon.
Also there's the 'Pediscope'
devoid, thank God, of isotope,
and arrow-heads from Cribden,
and a mangle, and a broom.

Weavers kiss their shuttles
in salute of silver trowels
used by philanthropic aldermen
to lay their firms' foundation.
Bequeathed to all are slubbing bobbins,
odd stacks of pyrites brick,
and strikers' bonds from Haslingdeners
locked out of the mill.

Summer: Whittaker Park.

Happily, snappily, instant holidays: trotting up the bridleway
to Whittaker Park; making overtures to ladybirds, and rude
remarks to raspberries; all innocent and winsome on the
swings and roundabouts.

There's a treadmill and a space rocket, a gibbet and a wobbly
globe, a Moebius strip of ladders, and a lopped log
thing'mabob. There are treasured wrecks of BMX lain
scuttled in the bushes, but there's penknives and a reel of
cat-gut just right for the job.

A mottled den of conifers is slit with brassy hoverflies:
vibrating bands of copper highlight; energy and stasis. Great
whirligigs twirl earthward, frightening frogs the size of
thumbnails, clipping conkers girt with gruesome spikes like
medieval maces.

Tiaras of azaleas look nearly real as plastic, but the
groundsman thinks it's formal and he's never heard of 'twee'.
The monkey-puzzle's not fussed either, not about things
floral: it's that bit of so-called sculpture... *'what in hell's it
supposed to be?'*

Autumn: Stacksteads.

Pitched beneath the rake of rhododendrons and heather, where pipits pose questions and wolf-spiders cast their nets in the dew, dark rivulets scutter like phantom rats down trackless tunnels of rotting mortar.

In the husks of King Cotton corrugation now rules; provisional structures of lean-to tin sprout behind screens of spindle trees. By composite columns, under rickety rooves, the proud poor struggle to earn scant respect.

Pushed along paths to the rushing road, multiple mothers bounce babies at bus stops, warm laughter bubbles in popular pie shops, and grey old grannies in gay rayon head-scarves root among remnants of drab corner stores.

Past crazy galleries of skeletal scaffold and the furtive discharge of incontinent pipes, men walk dogs, or lean on pitted handrails, telling the thankless screeds of memory, or reckoning the benefits of joblessness.

Back Handyman's Warehouse, in close knit houses, kitchens full of kettles and bacon tea-cakes are crowded with cushions and next-door's cat. Here even fools know that there's smooth where there's rough:

> In the quiet of the grave
> There'll be room right enough.

Autumn: Cowpe.

Smashed by the Ice Giant's massive fist,
the fields of Cowpe are crumpled baize,
riven and ripped by spattering sheep:
a brutally murdered billiard table,
lying in a ring of flinders.

Amongst terminal tangle
and the entrails of tractors,
deranged dogs rattle their chains and chew planks,
whilst kittens hunt shrews,
robins scold wrens,
and a milk of mist rises to dilute the cobalt sky.

Hogging the head of the valley,
at Boarsgreave,
a yarn dyers hums on a stiltwork of conduits;
oaken doors lean open
to admit a glimpse of fireclay,
but spiders spin gossamer locks on the gate.

Lofted high above the ramparts of the reservoir
shelters, unshielded, yield to despair.
Deep in the roots and the ruins of resolve
like outcast wraiths of incestuous love
two sycamores intertwine.

Winter: Rawtenstall Market.

Armed with elbows and umbrellas,
talking turnips and tripe,
a reconnaissance in strength
of the fur-bootee battalion,
barge bits and bats of budgie cages,
ponder piles of out-size smalls,
and hold impromptu 'at homes'
in the middle of the aisle.

Eyes agog and gobs agape,
infant Hitlers slaver,
savouring the plenitude
of penny chews and treats.
Bulging bags of broken biscuits
bounce against the babies' ear muffs.
Pulses quicken, cot toys whisper:
'Hush, it's market day!'

In the closely coughing café
ancient fag-ends taint the tea.
Grimacing groups of garrulous granddads
greedily gum their dumpling broth,
while someone's nan,
with a flare for the foreign,
lards thick brown sauce
on her quiche and chips.

A hallowed ham is sacrificed
in ear-shot of profane advice:
the bawdy butchers asking ladies
how they like their meat!
Alongside, connoisseurs of fresh boiled beet
and cheese that smells like sweaty feet,
besiege the mounds of fruit and veg.
or throng the Stilton stall.

Grim girded,
up there in the ceiling,
Father Time ticks with conviction,
but is graced with less importance
than the queue for potted beef.
Just as the perfect mannered Pathan shows,
when Christian women buy his clothes:
'the varp is all vithin the veft'.
It is... it's market day.

Winter: The East Lancashire Railway

Pushchairs, bobble hats, an odour of anoraks, enamelled signs
for mustard, and red buckets full of sand: an authentic
coal-fired waiting room is fringed with ornate soffit board,
and manned by expert volunteers in jumbled uniforms.

Blinking into brand new viewcams, hyperactive absent fathers
are recording the arrival of the Santa Claus Express: cheering
compartments of urchins in antlers compete with trombones,
sending twiddling fingers fiddling with the dire display of
decibels as dazzling knots of day-glo jerkins clog the
tele-zoom.

The winter world slips backwards in relaxed and regal
splendour to the tramping yelp of leaf-springs and the
huffa-puffa beat. Transported by the tales of salt in little twists
of indigo, a brightly waving grandson absorbs history through
his seat.

The last train comes and night-dark smoke plumes blue within
grey within blue within grey. The faces on the footplate of the
fluid amber fire-box are painted with heat, as intense as
Vermeer. Sparks spin from a brazier as the crimson
guard's-lamp flickers, and imaginary stationmasters hurry
home for tea.

Winter: Rooley Moor Road.

Across the russet moss, striated by couch-grass and scumbled with snow, a sole surviving insect pursues a shaft of sunlight toward the boundary markers and the track-ways of the dead: into the land where walls disperse, impermanent as vapour trails, and mountains have been levelled to the sea.

Here Hades Hill stands, hard as hunger - nourished on the bones of men - and Neolithic labyrinths of mine-workings and pack-horse trails are home only to lichen and the random spoor of savages whose traffic cones or burnt-out bikes lie mangled in the scree.

Extinct quarries brim with silence joined in crystal grains of frozen shale; stalactites of ice cascade from fissures in the rock. The failing colours dwindle slowly like a long discarded etching, and the withered wind blows keenly with the constancy of hate.

Yet onward march the ragged flag-stones: rude and reeling in their glory; hopelessly defiant to the crude and crumbling core. And everywhere is water, sweeping over blackened shoals of peat, to run in rutted rivers down the roads of Rooley Moor.

TEDDY BANANAS

Alison M. Abel

Teddy Bananas

When Amelia's bedroom ceiling fell she was in Mr Patel's all-night grocery store, buying cigarettes. This was fortunate, for normally she would have been in bed at that time, and most of the ceiling fell on Amelia's bed. She had stayed up to watch a late-night discussion on television about the increasing cost of domestic fuel. Amelia's distress during the programme had been fed by alarm at the gas bill she had received that morning and a confused sense of betrayal that the speaker representing the party she believed to be on the side of people like her (the 'genteel poor' was a phrase she favoured for its combined overtones of solidarity and breeding) appeared bent on increasing the increase. She had expressed her emotions in deep inhalations and much flicking of ash and grinding of stubs.

And so it was that Amelia had run out of cigarettes and, anticipating a sleepless night, was across the road in Mr Patel's shop and not beneath the bedroom ceiling when it fell, although Amelia's bed was, and, on the bed, Teddy Bananas.

Amelia returned to the flat and sat hunched beside the unlit gas fire, preferring deprivation to mere economy. She drew her long dark cape around her. Tomorrow she would attempt a balance between her pension and her outgoings, make lists of all she bought and did not need, assess the warming power of a therm. She pondered the cost of heating the kettle for a hot-water bottle and, considering this, glanced towards the bedroom and saw, through the narrow opening of the door, the floor strewn with ceiling.

At first she did not understand what had happened, and thought vaguely of burglars. But the bilious glow from the street-lamp outside the bedroom window was sufficient to illuminate the truth, and a small, further fall behind the door - preventing access - was an unnecessary emphasis.

She knew. Even before she lifted the boxfile from the shelf, she knew; she knew as she scrabbled through the papers; and reading the document merely confirmed that knowledge. She was not insured for the descent of a ceiling.

Amelia lay on the floor, narrow and rigid along the seat cushions from the fireside chairs, staring at the living-room ceiling and not caring if it, too, were to fall. She thought of Teddy Bananas, entombed, Pompei-like, between the ceiling and the bed. She had not slept without him for nearly sixty years. She thought of the gas bill, and of all the bills to come. She thought of the inadequacy of her pension and her lack of capital. She had looked on saving as a lower-middle class activity and had despised the habit accordingly. Now she was surprised at the efficiency with which she devised a savings plan.

By dawn the plan was complete. Amelia rose from the cushions and took from the bureau drawer two sheets of lilac paper; a quantity of postcards, each printed with a faint pencil sketch of Aberdovey; the parish council minute book; and a flat red tin with a label, "PC only", glued to the lid. On one sheet of lilac paper she wrote in green felt pen: 1) Economise; 2) Save for Ceiling; 3) Liberate TB; 4) Save, Save, Save; and (in view of the speculation and gossip which she anticipated would welcome her plight) 5) Keep It Quiet and 6) Lie Low. She sellotaped this list to the front of the gas fire for maximum impact.

On the back of each postcard she wrote: "Wintering in Wales. Weather mixed", and addressed the cards to those of her acquaintances she considered most likely to seek her out. On the second sheet of lilac paper she wrote: "Dear Vicar, Gone away. Resignation herewith. A. Lawson, Secretary". She attached this note to the minute book with a rubber band. From the red parish council tin she took sufficient postage stamps for the Aberdovey postcards, writing "I owe God 7 2nd class" on a slip of paper she kept in the tin.

Then she went out into the grey light, to the postbox down the street, to the vicarage in the square, and for the second time to Mr Patel's all-night grocery store. She bought several more packets of cigarettes, milk, bread, a number of tinned items, a packet of digestive biscuits and a small block of plastic-sealed cheese, negotiating with Mr Patel a reduced price for the latter on the basis of its just-expired sell-by date. Experimentally, and successfully, she paid by cheque.

As she stacked her food for the week on the kitchen shelf Amelia congratulated herself on the competence with which she was dealing with the situation. If she could pay Mr Patel by cheque she need never risk meeting someone she knew in the high street, for her pension was paid directly into her bank account.

In the weeks that followed Amelia refined, but did not deviate from, her plan. One morning the telephone rang. Alarmed, she hid in the folds of her cape - she wore it always now, for warmth - and later that day arranged for the line to be disconnected. When a reminder came that her television licence was due for renewal she borrowed a stamp from God and wrote to say she no longer had a television. Thereafter she was troubled by thoughts of detector vans and TV investigators, until she had the idea of taping a piece of card across the screen and removing the plug. Soon after, the battery on her radio expired. She thought of the ceiling fund and did not buy another, although she missed the familiar voices reading the news, the World Service and the daily reassurance of 'The Archers'.

The weather became colder. Amelia drew the long dark curtains and spent more time on the cushions with coats, jackets and rainwear from the hallstand piled over her for warmth. She still wore the clothes she had been wearing the night the ceiling fell. She grieved for Teddy Bananas. There were times when her nerve almost failed and she longed to tell someone so they could tell her that she was doing well. Nevertheless, she shopped only at night, for in truth she now dreaded chance meetings with anyone, stranger or friend. With Mr Patel, neither friend nor stranger, but dignified, remote, like a doctor or priest, Amelia was almost at ease. She became adept at unearthing from his shelves dented tins, torn packaging, bruised fruit and out-of-date bacon on which she and Mr Patel agreed terms. The increasing presence of such items at the front of shelves and cabinets caused her from time to time to suspect collusion, but Mr Patel's quiet presence behind the till gave no sign of complicity.

Sometimes at night she would stand behind the curtains, parting their heavy folds a little to see across the street the glowing square of Mr Patel's grocery store and a miniature Mr Patel, like a doll, behind the till. When coloured lights appeared around the shop window Amelia knew that it would soon be Christmas. The night there were no lights, no golden glow, only darkness, she opened a tin of pilchards and wished Teddy Bananas a happy Christmas through the bedroom door, and a happy birthday too, for he had arrived at Christmas and she had loved him for his sad eyes, his yellow softness and his strangely incurving limbs.

After Christmas the weather worsened. The flat was bitterly cold. Now Amelia seldom left her bed of cushions and ate less to avoid shopping for more. One night, when hunger and lack of cigarettes finally drove her outside, she felt a great tiredness and lay down on the pavement. Mr Patel, recognising as Amelia the ragged heap across the street, telephoned for an ambulance.

Watching its blue halo depart, he did not expect the elderly lady to return. There would be no problem in re-letting the flat. He had not mentioned that he owned the building opposite, taking pleasure in the relationship of shopkeeper and customer more than in that of landlord and tenant, and in the secret, too. Tomorrow he would call the managing agents and ask them to send someone round to assess how much redecoration was needed. Technically that was the tenant's responsibility, but he doubted her estate would be large enough to meet the cost. Structural repairs were the landlord's. He did not anticipate any major work being necessary - she had been such a refined, self-effacing tenant - and the insurance would cover whatever might have to be done. Mr Patel picked up a wire basket and began moving slowly up and down the aisles of his shop, filling the basket with out-of-date goods.

***

It was very quiet in the high white room where Amelia slept, woke, and slept again. In her waking, she stretched along the strange familiarity of the bed and saw that the ceiling had been repaired and, like the walls, painted a cold, flat white. Once, screwing her eyes against the pale point of light in the ceiling, she wondered if the fitting were not a little modern for a bedroom. Later, she turned her head on the pillow and puzzled that there should be a window in the door. Turning her gaze once more to the ceiling, she wondered where Teddy Bananas was. She closed her eyes against the swirling light and drew her legs upwards and outwards a little, curving them to a reassuring shape. She could not remember what had happened to him, but she knew, wherever he was, he would be all right. He, like her, was a survivor.

PERSONAL COMPUTING

Pippa Meek

Poets

They pick up what they can
here and there. They have their
ear to the ground, watch chimney
pots from the corner of their eyes.
Make mental notes on the choreography
of pigeons. Sneak up on the wind.
That tree reminds them of something.
A raindrop is like? Is like? And what
is the weight of air upon the head?
What did that daffodil just say?

Like foxes or goblins they are
invisible amongst the busy lives.
Like children they deliberately
test the cracks for bears. Like
scientists, they observe at 2 a.m.
that the pavement is listening hard,
and places precise footsteps against
each falling foot. They are waiting
for the world to make a slip - for
a true secret to leak out - for tables
to walk, or crows to speak.

Waiting for those moments when
(although nobody else notices)
it rains kindnesses all over men,
or an angel can be seen, blowing and
waving in the sky above the Thames.

Personal Computing

My computer crashed when you
put your joystick near my laptop.
Wordwrap me on your spreadsheet -
our softwear is compatible.

They warned me that you are a multi-user -
a corrupted motherboard - a WIMP interface.
But then you loaded your floppy disk
into my hardwear, and used your mega-drive.

Download the body of your text
onto my screen. I want you to indent me,
and put me on your drop down list.
Look me up on the address bus.
Let's merge headers, and select options.

Before you inserted your data,
I was a standalone work station -
with an 8 bit 4, random access memory.
But you opened and saved a lost file
and turned on my bubble-jet.

So, move your cursor to *enter* -
double click on the space bar -
undelete me,
and I will produce multiple colour copies
in *italics*, and **bold**.

Balquidder Valley (I)

Washday in the pines:-
A warm wind blowing
from East to West.

Polluted words
exhausted from the world
are flowing in.

The hoovering
of an aeroplane
inside a cloud.

The protesting pain
of a sawdust drill
on upper slopes.

Clouds brush
the mountain tops
in their velvet upholstered green.

The small machinery of a busy bird -
squeaking wheels
on a nearby branch.

Loch Voil sucks her stony teeth.
The flies are lazy here
and not afraid.

Torrents of sound:-
the mountains are clapping.

Balquidder Valley (II)

That old mountain
is dribbling rocks again
rusting with crumbling bracken.

Its thin felt skin
can no longer cover
its angular granite joints.

The loch is slick, black and oily -
silky smooth and sticky as treacle -
its surface finely creased
as boiled sugar.

Sprinkled with granulated light.
Glamorous with electrical sequins.

Living so close for so many years -
loch and mountain are deeply silent
with pent up passion.

Found Poem

Walking evenly and smoothly
from the shrine room -
careful not to spill a word.

Zen master fly

Zen master fly, you have confounded me.

This morning you woke me up to meditate
at seven twenty one a.m.
by landing on my nose.

At first I tried to chase you
out - but like a demon,
you were not attracted to the light.

When I was meditating,
you crawled all over my gently folded hands:-
I could feel your sooty footfalls.

I poured the white light
of the Buddha's compassion upon you,
and *tried* to do it gently.

For much of the morning,
I wandered around the flat
with a red plastic sieve in my hands.

I finally gave up,
and took a good look at you -
prancing about my forearm

on your tiny eyelash feet.
Skittering over a surface as nifty
as a wrestler in roller skates -

or a bruiser in a nightie.
Light as a feather:-
boozy, bombastic, ballerina.

94

I ask
What is the sound of one hand clapping?
You ponder this by rubbing your legs in front.

I ask
Does the fly have Buddha nature? ...

You stare at me with satin bulbs for eyes,
roll out a party-pooper tongue
give me a tiny kiss.

Playing Houses

Our dolls house is a slum,
but we make our own
out of blankets and chairs
and pegs off the line.

We crawl in and crouch
in our separate caves,
for a long time not speaking.
Watching the light, through blanket holes.

When I lie to go to sleep
I imagine that the whole house is flooded
and I'm floating down the stairs on my bunk,
and floating out the door.

At school we learn
that houses can be made of bricks and wood.
They can be made with hay or dry twigs,
rags, clay or mud.

Later we learn
that some people's houses are made with air:
Their eyes are the windows -
and anyone can look in.

Ideas, but not the thing itself.

The idea of *getting* married
is the only thing about getting married
that I like:-

To have a big party,
To get dolled up,
To have my cake,
To dance a lot.

Invite my friends and relatives -
the main ones, and the strange ones -
watch as all the parts of my life
step towards each other
and eye each other up -
over
over-flowing glasses.

The *idea* of having children
is the only thing about having children
that attracts me:-

I'd like it to stay as snapshots;
Us on a beach near Dover,
Us in funny hats in France.
The beautiful couple and baby
meander down a street -
entwined, complete.

Not those endless deserts in between
of boring conversations
and pulling their socks up.
Mummy - are we there yet?

Hourglass

Become aware of the breathing process -
just watching, and not trying
to change anything.

Ten minutes into it;
my body is an
hourglass.

I am
watching
each grain as it
falls through a narrow gap.

Each one so unique -
it brings tears to my eyes.

Thief

Stealing from the shrine room -
precious words. Later
I sift through them -
hunched, and leafing the pages.

Come back - listen harder

If you let go of everything
and lie absolutely still
just breathing
like an animal in the wilderness,
surely the universe will send an answer.

This is how it is at 3 a.m.,
staring up at stars
that stare back, hard,
reflecting your fiery questioning.

You might make a decision:-
OK - nobody cares -
I don't believe in anything.

And turn away -
step into the night, alone:-
live the rest of your life
hidden, in the babble of a radio set,
or the glare of a T.V. screen -
letting other people
run your secret dreams.

Otherwise, you might expand
into the enormous no-reply
of the Universe -

hear that silence pouring from
the closed mouths of all things -
and glimpse transcendence
in the reflection of your own face.

The fridge

All is well if the fridge is humming -
It is allowed to shudder and make
Funny noises - like a well humoured uncle.
It is the heart, the living heart of a
Flat or house, when you are alone.

You go to it for nourishment at night
At the loneliest hours. It shines
Its light out at you and hums
Into the dark. It is so full of milk
That it weeps milk rivers under the door.

No monsters will come as it hums.
No matter that it's cool, it wants nothing
Back - it is not sentimental but solid
And upstanding. Like a tiny incubator
It keeps alive our lonely little needs.

At night pay obeisance on your knees
To each humble lit up shrine.
A hollow black silence may be pressing
At the doors. But all is well
If the fridge is still humming.

Couple on a bench at Clapham Junction.

She's a made-up blonde in heels and a dress -
drawing the dregs from a cigarette.
Then the voice again - *You make me sick -
d'you hear me... make me bloody sick...*

She sneers it loudly - slurred and hoarse -
sloppily leaning towards the boy, who takes
the words like a breaking wave - his eyebrows
and shoulders slightly raised.

Then he seems to be talking in measured tones -
laying out reasons with open palms - and he
looks like a smart little diplomat in his
school kit, trainers and naff naff bag -

trying to get her to climb the stairs whilst
she's sitting and swaying and dropping her purse.
(With legs held together and eyes fixed as birds' -
you can tell she's trying to catch his words.)

I take a look at my business-man neighbour -
who looks straight ahead, and then unfolds his paper.
My train arrives, and I board it, sober -
getting a view of the boy, and his mother.

From here I can see from his face that he's older -
but lifting her bag over unfledged shoulders.
Something's not shared as the train moves off,
and I feel ashamed to have witnessed love.

FLIGHT OF THE BIN BAGS

Jean Barker

Grandmother's Plant Pot

... bears a scar from rim to base,
a war wound worn with pride,
earned in a London blitz
when it lay broken on her rug.

When the bomb screamed down
I cowered under her table.
The cat's green eyes met mine
glowing with reciprocal terror
from under the kitchen range.

She gave her best bedspread
to shroud the body by the gate;
blood stained its pristine whiteness
(proof of hours at the washtub)
but it couldn't hide my first horror
of death by violence.

Later I passed gaping houses,
pictures still in straight lines
as though hung for a street viewing.
My mother said four died there
sitting round the dining table.
She said our next door neighbour
held a winning hand of cards.

Gran mended the Romantic scene
decorating her heirloom -
a gift from an uncle in Dresden.

Today I get my violence from T.V.
Crying women in ruined streets -
Beirut, Baghdad, Bosnia.
Dead children or rape victims,
all feed the voyeur's palate.

I value grandmother's plant pot -
ironically it holds a peace-lily.
Her old repair holds good
but a crack still splits Romantic skies
like a long shaft of lightning -
it points to the chasm open at my feet.

Moon

Skies range from sapphire to violet.
She hides her rotundity in shadow,
releases her new-born
to lie   feet up
in the dark arms of the tree.
Nights pass.
She reveals her comeliness
to shine for her lover, Earth;
later she cloaks again in darkness -
secretly prepares for another birth.

Survivors

Children -
we played in ruined streets,
wondered how fennel and willowherb
grew so quick over rubble:
or in broken churches
with ghosts   recalled to our shattered City
by guns of nightly conflict.

Adolescents -
we met in our Enemy's ruins
where stench of death and brickdust
crept with the living from cellars.
We longed for London bombsites,
London-pride   cafés
smells of the Underground.

In Germany -
we still found wildflowers.
Buttercup   groundsel   ragwort
poked through stone and plaster -
seeded on broken Rathaus roofs.
We loved on the daisied riverbank
after hearing the Siegfried Idyll.

Today
I heard you were dead
from a cause as common as cancer -
and wondered at our chance survival.
Now, fed images of current warfare
from Iraq or Sarajevo,
I wonder if the young still love
amid wonder of returning wildflowers
where ruins loom through dusk.

At Notre-Dame

In the cool shade
of this great Cathedral
I lit a candle
for you - dead -
in half my years.

It swelled the glow
from hundreds
and the kaleidoscopic colours
of stained glass
revealed in dusty sunbursts.

How many mothers
performed this act
for sons lost
in Crusades - Revolutions
or Wars to End Wars,

praying that somehow
their small flame still glows
waiting to spring up
swell and blaze
at the heart of the Spirit?

Behold the Woman

Lying prone amid upright sculptures,
this is no Florentine Nativity -
a marbled girl holding well fleshed child
under a halo of innocence.

This blue wrap is threadbare, dusty,
it covers her skeleton. She lies dying
on iron hard earth, where torn feet
carried despair to this final solution.

Her manchild is locked on wrinkled breasts
his silent wail and stick legs speak his story.
Today the child is crucified
before the family reaches Egypt.

Herod is redundant.

Written after seeing the Zimbabwean sculpture
'Desperate Mother' at the West Yorkshire Sculpture Park (1990)

Between Times

Midnight. We leave the Cathedral
to an air-splitting peal of celebratory bells
welcoming New Year.

Outside our breath steams upward
as we stamp, clap, chatter,
jostle to light flares from a burning brazier.

We march to the Town Square, laughing.
Torches reek, acrid smoke pricks throats,
laddish youths jeer from high branches.

Suddenly the crowd turns -
flames and bodies circle closer
and I am cold, cold inside.

"Why do you live alone with a cat?
Are your runes from the Devil?
Do your spells kill babies, sicken cattle?"

Flares flickerlight grinning faces,
the press tightens, sleet needles eyes.
Sightless I struggle, break free.

I stand and shiver on Cathedral steps
where boys tend a dying brazier;
bells renew their peal to faith in the future.

My friend's smiling face appears,
"Oh, there you are,
I've been looking everywhere for you -

we all thought you were lost."

Home

My spirit craves old houses
characters in brick or stone
not modern, new wood,
new-paint-smelling
unlived-in units.

I love rooms that creak, groan
whisper of the past
as I love Grandma's art-pot
or Mother's cheap but pretty
Chinese jars;

these link me to tough roots,
London of the 'forties blitz,
of my immigrant forebears
or nineteenth century
Romantic Germany.

I need the feel of times gone,
to belong in homes
inhabited by ghosts
who lived, loved, fought -
struggled to survive.

My father fucked and fled,
left a gap in my story.
Like a three legged table
in need of a prop
this sense of place upholds me.

Old houses make poetry,
floorboards crack and settle,
rooms exhale strange music.
The blackened steeple looks down
clothed in working grime

and I belong.

New Living

I'm going to live under a glass dome
with a beautiful lemon tree
and a black cat
with yellow eyes and silken fur.
I'll drink cherry-brandy
eat dark chocolate with soft centres.
Take an afternoon lover.

In the cool of evening
I'll write poems
about parrots, rainbows and love;
listen to the sea
whispering secrets to the shoreline,
feel the movement of the turning world.
Learn about myself.

Trapped in the System (For Mary Sheepshanks)

"Go left," I say.
"I can't," she says,
"The signpost says Go Right."
Trapped in the one-way system
we go on turning right
and right again
moving further from our goal.

Like my life, I think.
I want to sit at my desk
and write memorable poems.
"Come and work for the Party,"
says one. "You know it's important."
"We need you on the P.C.C."
says another. "You're reasonably articulate."

"The Playhouse is over there"
I point left.
She says we must keep going right
as the sign directs
so we drive up Hunslet Road
on the way out of Town.
Like my politics, I think,
I aim Left and am pulled Right
but I still keep going.

All my life I tried to go one way
and was directed another.
My social achievements are puny
and I have a few bad poems.
Now I travel to the country
when I want to be in Town...

"I think I'll do a U-turn,"
she says.

Flight of the Bin Bags

Liberated by gales
from under bin lids
we fly   tumbling
flapslapping over cyclists.

We move in unison
over City streets
threatening   becoming
an alien force.

We will no longer
be equated with rubbish.
With our ally the wind
we dash for freedom.

Tomorrow early
black flags of anarchy
will flutter from branches
challenging all things.

Extravaganza

Tucked in a terrace of small houses
it functions to help the aged
with 'forties bric-a-brac,
tired suits, yellowing lampshades
and tacky browning paperbacks.
I feel weighed down with old.

Look up. Hanging from dark rafters -
exotic underwear, revealing, erotic.
The briefest of briefs rub gussets
with calf-length frilly drawers;
boned red basques, black laced,
touch up flouncy petticoats.

I am spirited to Montmartre,
to the world of Toulouse Lautrec
to paint charity-shop ladies
who kick high, draw wide circles
with toes of lace up boots.
They flash frou-frou skirts,
display frilled bottoms for posterity.

I draw the shop's till-guardian,
slim his beer-belly
into black drainpipe trousers.
He dons a battered opera hat,
dances for an evening's absinthe.
I paint to the music of the Moulin Rouge
a Nineteenth Century raffish glamour.

But friends lead me outside
talking of jam and the W.I. Market.
I walk through a world of discarded clothes,
disintegrating Archer novels -
and charity for the old -
to a new, empty millenium-domed Britain.

Miranda

You withheld your Art from me, Father,
magic man, manipulator of elements.
You taught me letters, obedience,
the importance of remaining a virgin
until you conjured me a brave new husband
from chaos of storm and sea change.
And I was happy, for that was a time
when hot young blood subdued the mind.
I made no protest when you broke your staff,
shattered my inheritance forever.
Now you are dead. My husband, grown fat,
spends his days at the legislature,
his nights with the Palace concubines.
My spirit flies like Ariel, from sea to sea
unanchored by skill with holding spell;
I have no craft to sail her to freedom.
Like Caliban, after he showed you
all the qualities of the island,
I am wracked, angry, at the mercy of fools.

Mother to the Woman

Perhaps it was walking beside you
as we walked that other Sunday,
first of the War, in autumn sunshine.

Perhaps the last scattered poppies,
blackberries, rib-caged willowherb,
brown dock or browning grass.

Perhaps it was the book you gave me -
tales of London evacuees, vulnerable,
lonely, labelled like excess baggage

that called up this waif before me,
weaving between us, brash, defiant,
secretly afraid of an unknown future.

Did we draw the thread of memory,
spin this cobweb child
who dances beside two ageing women

strolling in September sunlight,
remembering, laughing, still defiant -
secretly afraid of an unknown future?

ALWAYS, EVER, OTHERWISE

Jez Colclough

Foundation Year

Three whole months
drawing the same naked body.
From above, from below,
from the back, sitting down,
standing up, from the front;
with pencil, with crayon
we explored every fold,
every crook and every cranny.

Fulfilling each promise,
occasionally,
erasing every deceit
more often than not,
we learnt how to see
by drawing from life
because we had to see
to draw from our lives.

And then came colour,
our teacher standing at the front
with his six foot square
reproduction of the Hay Wain.
He invited us closer
and then we saw:

A canvas divided into squares,
and each square divided
into more squares
impossible to count.
Each tiny brick a building block
of one solid colour, one concrete hue.

And still,
I did not understand
until you took me
by the hand
and showed me how
a purple flower
might be concealed
within the blue
hint of your lips
and the burning
in your cheeks.

Love Token

You gave me a little
black man made of steel,
with two holes in his head
for eyes and a crescent moon
where his mouth should have been
but the most remarkable thing about
this man is the hole in his chest that is shaped
like a heart, and lately, long after the time
for such tokens has past,
I find myself wondering who took it? And why
that it is, that I have come to care so much
for this little black man
with a hole in his chest
where his heart should have been.

Moments

Introduction:

I shall close me eyes,
Pretend this is an innocent childhood game
of hide and seek.
Count one through ten.

1. Invisible Ink

How I spent each evening crushing onions
In our secret lovers game of hide and seek.

How you sat and gently warmed the page
until each browning word or phrase

revealed itself
beneath the naked flame.

How we always said,
We wouldn't get our fingers burnt.

How each night my fingers wrote their angry onion kiss
On fresh blank reams of new found skin.

How every onion cut
Now reeks of you.

How words break free,
Become a prison in this prisoner's game.

Jez Colclough

2. First Kisses

She stands up.
Says
"you can come in now",
passes me the towel
and wraps herself
within my outstretched arms.

It was a strangely tender
form of kissing;
hand through cloth
on shoulder, breast,
belly and thigh.
She said,
"yes,
that's right".

3. Birthday

The look on your partner's face,
When you asked me if I'd seen

Your birthday gifts.
Too close to the bone.

Too close to the skin the silk and satin
in that private, brief exchange.

The look on your partner's face
When you entered modelling them.

This childish game of hide and seek
Was killing him.

4. This light

We basked in the sight of summer's six a.m.
Sharing a journey towards different homes.

If I took your hand and explained how, as a child,
I was taught to kiss like butterflies and Eskimos,
It was because there is a sanctuary to be found
In laughter, and the innocence of childhood games.

And if the truth be told I was more than a little shaken by the light,
How naturally the moon took its place in the azure sky.

And this light was as bright as the midday sun
And the roads held their silence, like church mice.

5. Gifts

How I gave you a copy of Roget's,
Didn't tell you that on page

Three hundred and seventy eight
I had erased

Adore, cherish, desire,
worship, Et cetera...

had written
There is no substitute.

How I watched you leave again,
~~because you couldn't stay the night.~~

How you crossed out
the (Concise) Oxford English
definition of love,
put in its place

two letters, F and A
Your initials, a code.

A sweet summing up.

Epilogue

... six, seven,
eight, nine, ten.
Blink open,
blink shut,
blink open again.
Pretend this is an innocent's
Childhood game
of hide and seek.

Natural States

The kettle is switched on
then forgotten about,
left to fill the room
with a cloud of vapour
that would, under different
circumstances, be water. Returning

to his chair, He says
no, it is more soulful
than that. It is the friendship
we circle like wagons.
The way we protect one another
from each other. And the steam,
from the kettle, drifts and rises

feeling its way across to the window:
Cold glass streaming the tears
of that which, under different
circumstances, would be vapour.
She turns

to him and says
no, it is more sexual
than that. It's the aesthetic
we aspire to, it is the desire
we possess to possess what
we desire. And now
condensation
grasps the glass

that conducts the crisp night air:
icy breath, freezing the tears
of that which, under different
circumstances, would be liquid.

He says
no, it is more civic
than that, it is the tether,
the chord. The bond
that ties a parent to tomorrow,
and the child to yesterdays.

She stands and moves
towards the kettle,
half full of a liquid
that would, under different
circumstances be vapour,
be ice, be liquid again.

Lover

Sometimes I wear the
cardigan that used to belong
to my sister's dead lover and
think of dead men, but I have
worn it so often now it
just smells like me.

Capsize Drill

The sheets,
you gotta make sure
you've freed off the main.
Damn thing'll keep on sailing
If you don't, on her side
or not.
So you'll have to slow her down.

And keep with her.
Remember
you'll never get home
without her,
and arse over tit
she belongs to the tide
not you
anymore.

Most important of all
keep clear of the sails,
get trapped
beneath canvas
and you panic
and panic will kill you
quicker than exhaustion
or the cold.

But keep with her,
grab hold onto something
and keep with her.

These were my father's
only words of advice
and I hear them.

As my face hits the water
and cold rips the air
from my lungs
I hear them again.

I open my eyes,
spy the bottom of the bowl,
the plug in the hole,
raise my head
face myself
back to front
in the mirror.

I am home.

Back beneath the sheets
she says: "You are wet".
I grab hold.

Please

Don't touch me.
Please, don't touch me.

Instead, smile, laugh
lower your eyes

and sit on the bed
and try to pretend

it is not
what it is.

Don't kiss me.
Don't reach out your hand

and kiss me.
Don't invite that betrayal

Don't
even ask

Just leave.
And leave me tonight

with only a taste
of your scent on my pillow

and how I imagine a kiss
might have parted these lips.

But don't make me say no
until tomorrow and tomorrow

and tomorrow we can meet
and pretend

this is not
what it is.

More a tap than a thud

More a tap than a thud
the sound of the news down
the alley that splashes
old mud on new shoes.

Not late but enough to be
wondering if it is wise
to wander this way back home
late at night

tighter her breath when she hears
more thud than a tap
on the cobbles behind her and the light
in her head turns to green and she thinks
he should cross and find another way
home

quicker her steps and she thinks
will he notice though his own have grown
slower still louder and closer
and she hears like a mouse the sound of a zipper
and the hand sliding in past the zip to the pocket
at the end of the alley she runs, runs for cover
and I pass and I wonder who's behind me
a thudding my fist past the zip
in my pocket my fingers all wrapped
round my keys just in case they are
called on to stab or to blind those behind me
a calling more tap than a thud and the sound of old news down
the alley that splashes fresh mud on new shoes

November Mornings

Close your eyes.
Kneel

Reach out your hand
and feel the indifference of stone.

Let your fingertips trace
the pattern language makes.

Remember a name.
Exhale the ghost of a form

into cold morning air.
and remember a face.

Open your eyes.
See the grass

has grown back
and healed this once turned earth.

Notice how the trees appear
not to have changed.

But know
that they have

grown and moved
in a million tiny ways

since the last time
you came and we met.

128

BIOGRAPHICAL NOTES

Alison M. Abel

Born in Cheshire. For some 20 years worked as an Editor for a number of London publishers. Now a free-lance Editor. Started writing when she joined a creative writing class in 1994. In 1995 was a runner-up in the Ilkley Literature Festival Poetry Competition and won the Airedale Writers' Circle Overall Challenge Cup. Also reached the semi-finals of the One Voice 95 Monologue Competition. Her short story, 'Teddy Bananas' is the first of her works to appear in print.

Jean Barker

Born in Kilburn, N.W.London. Lived there until coming to Leeds in 1976. Has done many jobs, from Dinner Lady in school, Clerk in the Employment Exchange, WEA Tutor and Tutor/Counsellor for the Open University. Editor of poetry magazine *Aireings* from its inception in 1980, but for the last two years has been joint Editor with Linda Marshall. Has a son and family living in Norwich.

John Carley

Born in Manchester in the mid-fifties, he rejected a promising academic career to pursue his interests in music and travel. Has lived abroad extensively. Has published lyrics, translations and verse in English, French Italian, Piemontëis. Member of the Loose Leaf Writers' Co-operative, co-founder of Big Lamp Community Publishing and is compiling Editor of the *Pennine Ink* magazine.

Helen Clare

Taught biology for several years. Now working for Project one O one, a community literature project based in Haslingden, Lancs. Co-wrote 'The Seasiders', a soap opera commissioned and broadcast on BBC Radio Lancashire. Writes short stories and articles. Co-edits *Pennine Ink*, a small press magazine supported by Pennine Ink Writers' Workshop, Burnley. Lives in Rossendale with her husband, Peter, with whom she travelled to California last Spring.

129

Jez Colclough

Born in Newcastle-under-Lyme, 1973. Graduated with First Class Honours degree in English and Drama from St. Martin's College, Lancaster, in 1995. Completed an M.A. in Creative Writing at Bretton Hall, W.Yks. in 1997. His poetry has been published by *Staple New Writing* and *Framework Press*. Was placed joint-third in the Northern New Writers' Award for poetry, 1997. Is currently the Assistant Editor of *Pennine Platform*.

Josie Kildea

Born Cambridge. First public writing a winning essay on Cinema. She has 3 grown-up children, grandchildren and an encouraging husband. Maternal grandparents were a Catholic grandmother from Flemish stock and a Jewish grandfather. She is interested in what forms people. Her teaching experience has ranged from Montessori infant, secondary and comprehensive schools to prison work. Her personal interests are free dancing to jazz, life-drawing classes and, of course, writing - always "tracing the edges".

Pippa Meek

Born London, 1964. Grew up in Broughty Ferry, near Dundee, Scotland. Trained and worked as a social worker in Lancaster and Ipswich, during which time she discovered Buddhism. Moved to South London in 1989 to live and work with other Buddhists. Audible murmurings of poetry were being detected by 1996. Since then has designed her life to accommodate this. Lives alone and works part-time with people who have learning disabilities.

Lesley Quayle

Born Dunfermline, Fife. Brought up in Glasgow and, later, Margate, Kent. Father a Naval Officer. Married to a veterinary surgeon. Four children (including identical twins). They have a small farm where they breed Herdwick sheep. Her husband is a fine guitarist, and together they have run folk clubs and played and sung in them. Lesley plays the bodhran, bowed psaltery and guitar. Has had her poetry published in various magazines. Writes articles for the *Yorkshire Journal*, *Yorkshire Post* and *Tykes News*.

Alex Shaw

Born Otley, W.Yks. Brought up in nearby Horsforth. Educated at the University College of St. Martin (a College of Lancaster University). Tutors Basic Maths and English at Park Lane College, Leeds. Also writes advertisement brochures and magazine articles connected with the motor industry. He feels he is merely at the beginning of his writing career.

Duncan Earl Smith

Born S.Yks. 1930. Highly-qualified engineer. Served in the Royal Mechanical & Electrical Engineers as Artillery Artificer on attachment to the 32 Medium Regiment, Royal Artillery for 4 years, serving 2 years in the Middle East (Singapore and the New Territories on the border with China). Eventually, back in England, worked as a self-employed consultant Filtration Engineer covering the Northern Counties and Scotland. Now, he has almost completed an autobiographical account, 'Pearl of the Orient', that covers his experience of service life during the mid-fifties in the Far East.

Margaret Wainwright (Surtees)

Born Bradford, Yks. Educated at Hanson Primary School, Bradford Girls' Grammar School and Oxford. The decade 1950-1960 was spent teaching. From 1960-1970 she held a post with E.J.Arnold & Son Limited, Leeds, as Editor for Secondary English. A Poetry Course run by Jon Silkin at Leeds University initiated her serious writing of poetry. Published works include *All the Quiet People* (Outposts Publications, 1970) and contributions to *Pennine Platform*. In 1971 she married Derek Surtees. After his death she retired to Newcastle upon Tyne to live with a sister.

John Walker

Lives near Keighley, W.Yks. He is married, with three children. Founder member of the S.W.I.G. (Skipton Writers' Informal Group). This is his first collection of poems to appear in print.

131

ACKNOWLEDGEMENTS

Jean Barker

Aireings: 'Survivors', 'Between Times', 'Flight of the Bin Bags', 'Trapped in the System', 'New Living'

Blue Unicorn (USA), and *Aireings*: 'Miranda'

Pennine Platform and *Aireings*: 'Mother to the Woman'

Helen Clare

Smiths Knoll: 'Bolinas Beach'

Jez Colclough

Staple New Writing, Staple Press, 1996 and 1997: 'More a Tap Than a Thud', 'Foundation Year'

Northern New Writers' Awards Anthology, City of Sunderland College Press, 1997: 'November Mornings'

Josie Kildea

Rustic Rub: 'Stolen Walk', 'Friday's Walk'

Beyond Bedlam, Anvil Press, 1997: 'At the Braque Exhibition'

Pippa Meek

A Recollection of Legs, self published, 1997: 'Poem', 'Found Poem', 'Thief'

Margaret Wainwright

Pennine 25, Fighting Cock Press, 1991: 'Photographs of my Mother' (under married name Margaret Surtees)

All the Quiet People, Outpost Publications, 1970: 'For John Clare'

John Walker

Pennine Magazine: 'Jim Allen Lane'

Smiths Knoll: 'Snowprint', 'Dry Walling'

Pennine Platform: 'Cheyney is Fit'